20
Totally Awesome
& Totally Easy
Language Arts
Bulletin Boards

by Michael Gravois

SCHOLASTIC
PROFESSIONAL BOOKS

New York • Toronto • London • Auckland • Sydney
Mexico City • New Delhi • Hong Kong • Buenos Aires

Dedication

To Marsha Sykes,
who speaks the language of friendship

Cover design by Maria Lilja
Interior design by Michael Gravois
Interior and cover illustrations by Jim Palmer

ISBN 0-439-37076-0

Table of Contents

Introduction

About This Book

Too often bulletin boards are just thought of as *decoration*, when they really should emphasize the learning that is taking place in your classroom by displaying your students' work. These two qualities do not have to be mutually exclusive; a bulletin board can be both educational and decorative.

However, creating attractive and educational bulletin boards that enrich your classroom can be a difficult and time-consuming task. *20 Totally Awesome & Totally Easy Language Arts Bulletin Boards* makes this task easy for you by providing everything you'll need to create bulletin boards that focus on all areas of the language arts—from reading and writing to speaking and listening, with a strong emphasis on the visual arts.

Because these bulletin boards feature work that is mostly created by students, it not only saves you time, but it gives them a sense of ownership of the classroom by surrounding them with examples of their work. As a teacher, you only need to set up the bulletin boards and let students do the rest.

Using This Book

In this book, you'll find step-by-step directions for creating each bulletin board, as well as templates and reproducible student pages to make assembling the bulletin boards a snap!

20 Totally Awesome & Totally Easy Language Arts Bulletin Boards is designed so that you can pick and choose the projects that best connect with your curriculum. The table of contents lists the skills on which each bulletin board focuses. And with a little creative adapting, you can use these ideas across the curriculum.

Above all, use the ideas in this book to add a sense of fun to your classroom. Your students are sure to be engaged by the wide range of activities that these bulletin boards provide, which will keep their school days interesting, challenging, and fun. And a classroom in which students enjoy themselves is a classroom where learning is taking place.

Word Webs

Webbing activities take on new meaning as you create this fanciful bulletin board that is sure to delight students as they review the eight parts of speech.

Materials

* Spider template (page 6)
* Web template (page 7)
* Eight long strips of black paper
* 40 or more strips of white paper (about 2–3 inches long)

Creating the Bulletin Board

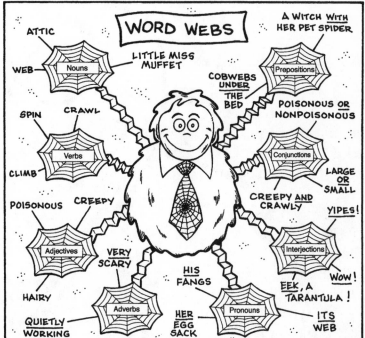

* Using the web template, copy and cut out the Spider template. Color the spider and then create legs by cutting long strips of paper. To make the legs appear three-dimensional, accordion-fold them. Staple the spider and the legs to your bulletin board.

* Copy and cut out eight spider webs. Write the name of a different part of speech on each web. Staple a web at the end of each of the spider's legs.

* Explain to the class what a graphic organizer is and that a word web is a type of graphic organizer used for brainstorming.

* Review the parts of speech with students. Then, as a class, brainstorm examples of each part of speech. If you'd like, have the class relate the words to a theme that you are studying (such as spiders, insects, or Halloween), but this is not necessary. Use the following prompts to encourage students:

  Nouns: People, places, and things associated with spiders (Little Miss Muffet, attic, web)
  Verbs: Actions associated with spiders (spin, crawl, climb)
  Adjectives: Words that describe spiders (creepy, hairy, poisonous)
  Adverbs: Spider-related phrases containing adverbs (*very* scary, *quietly* working)
  Pronouns: Spider-related phrases containing pronouns (*his* fangs, *her* egg sac, *its* web)
  Prepositions: Prepositional phrases about spiders (cobwebs *under* the bed, a witch *with* her pet spider)
  Interjections: Spider-related sentences that begin with an interjection (*Eek*, a tarantula!)
  Conjunctions: Conjunctions that join two similar words related to spiders (creepy *and* crawly, large *or* small, poisonous *or* nonpoisonous)

* Write the words and phrases on strips of white paper and staple them near the appropriate spider web.

* Add a banner that reads WORD WEBS.

Word Webs Web template

Eye Spy Nouns

Send students on a treasure hunt as they search for common and proper nouns to add to a class-made collage.

Materials

* Banner templates (pages 9 and 10)
* 6 large sheets of poster board
* old magazines
* 6 different colored markers or pens
* 6 pairs of scissors
* 6 glue sticks

Creating the Bulletin Board

◆ Copy and cut out the six banners on the Banner templates.

◆ Glue one banner onto each of the six sheets of poster board.

◆ Divide the class into six groups, and have a separate work station for each group.

◆ Give each group one of the sheets of poster board, a stack of old magazines, a colored marker or pen, a pair of scissors, and a glue stick.

◆ Each group will have three or four minutes to find pictures in their magazines that illustrate the type of noun featured on their poster board. They should cut out each picture, glue it onto the poster, and write the noun that the picture represents at the bottom of the poster board. The groups can decide which student(s) will have each job (searcher, cutter, gluer, writer).

◆ When you call time, each group should take their colored marker and their magazines to the next station. Again, give them three or four minutes to find as many pictures as possible that illustrate the type of noun featured on that poster board.

◆ Continue this process until each group has stopped at each of the six stations.

◆ At the end of this activity you will have six noun collages featuring common and proper nouns: people, places, and things. The color-coded markers make it easy for you to know which nouns were added by each group. Check their work to make sure there are no mistakes. If you find a mistake, have the group cross it out and rewrite it correctly.

◆ Create a banner that reads: EYE SPY NOUN COLLAGES—CAN YOU FIND THE NOUNS? Hang the posters in the hallway so that other students can try to find the different nouns listed on each poster.

COMMON NOUNS
PEOPLE

PROPER NOUNS
PEOPLE

COMMON NOUNS
PLACES

PROPER NOUNS
PLACES

COMMON NOUNS
THINGS

PROPER NOUNS
THINGS

Singular Sensations

This bulletin board can be displayed throughout the year as an educational reference for students.

Materials

* Rules list (page 12)
* Singular/Plural template (page 13)
* 7 sheets of poster board
* scissors
* glue sticks
* colored pencils or markers

Creating the Bulletin Board

* Give each student a copy of the Rules list, and review the seven rules for changing singular nouns to plural nouns.

* Divide the class into seven groups, and assign one rule to each group.

* Give each group a sheet of poster board. They should lay it in front of them vertically and write their rule across the top of the poster board using bold, creative letters.

* Have each student complete a copy of the Singular/Plural template. Then ask students to write a singular and plural noun that illustrates their rule and draw a colorful picture above each noun.

* Following the directions at the bottom of the template, they should fold their pages along the dotted lines, so that the top and bottom edges form long tabs.

* Finally, have them glue both Tab A's to their poster board so that their illustration of the rule stands out from the poster.

* Hang the posters on a wall in the classroom so students can refer to them throughout the year. Add a banner that reads SINGULAR SENSATIONS.

NAME: _____

R ule #1

To change most nouns from singular to plural, just add -s.
Examples: girl/girls, lion/lions, bug/bugs

R ule #2

Add -es to nouns that end in s, ss, sh, ch, x, or z.
Examples: dress/dresses, fox/foxes, church/churches

R ule #3

**If a noun ends in a consonant followed by -y,
change the y to i and add -es.**
Examples: baby/babies, pony/ponies, lady/ladies

R ule #4

If a noun ends in a vowel followed by -y, just add -s.
Examples: monkey/monkeys, boy/boys, tray/trays

R ule #5

**For most nouns that end in an -f or -fe,
change the f or fe to v and add -es.**
Examples: knife/knives, leaf/leaves, wolf/wolves
Exceptions: roof/roofs, giraffe/giraffes

R ule #6

Some nouns change their spelling to form the plural.
Examples: foot/feet, child/children, tooth/teeth

R ule #7

Some nouns remain the same for both singular and plural.
Examples: moose/moose, deer/deer, sheep/sheep

Tab A

Tab B

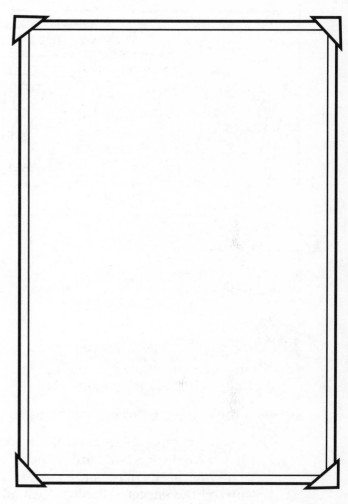

SINGULAR

PLURAL

Tab B

Fold Tab A behind Tab B. Fold Tab B behind your illustration. Do the same to the upper tabs. Glue both Tab A's to your poster so your illustration pops out.

Tab A

Tomorrow, Today Will Be Yesterday

Send students on a creative writing journey
through their past, present, and future
as they explore different verb tenses.

Materials

* Writing template (page 16)
* colored pencils
* glue sticks
* construction paper

Getting Started

♦ Discuss the fact that verbs not only tell the reader or listener *what* is being done, but also *when* the action is taking place.

♦ Read the following three paragraphs to the class:

Past—Last spring I spent several days working on the garden in my front yard. First, I turned the flower bed with a shovel and added nutrients to the soil. Next, I scattered wildflower seeds across the surface and tamped them into the soil. Then, I carefully watered the garden. Finally, I waited with anticipation.

Present—The garden in the front yard is bursting with color and life. Flowers of every shade create a display that causes people to stop and enjoy the beauty. A humming-bird visits the honeysuckle vine that climbs along the porch railing. The sweet scent of the blossoms floats through the air. Nature is truly awesome.

Future—In the fall, the green leaves will turn brown, the frost will kill the annuals, and the perennials will wait for the spring to return. Squirrels will bury their nuts in the earth. The foliage will decompose, which will add nutrients to the soil. Snow will cover the flower bed and offer protection from the harsh winds. I will look out the window of my warm house and plan next year's garden.

♦ Ask students how they can tell *when* the action in these three paragraphs takes place. Have them identify the verbs in the paragraphs and note the differences.

♦ Ask students to pick a topic about which they could write three paragraphs—one set in the past tense, one in the present tense, and one in the future tense. You might ask the class to brainstorm topics together, or you might ask students to write three paragraphs about themselves—what they were like a few years ago, what they are like now, and where they envision themselves in another 10 or 20 years. Have them write their draft copies and then edit them.

♦ Give each student two copies of the Writing template.

♦ They should cut the pages in half along the dotted line (figure 1). Each student will need three halves. They can use the fourth half as a backup in case they make a mistake.

♦ Next, ask students to place the writing templates in front of them so the dashed line is at the bottom.

♦ Have them fold the small bottom strip upwards and crease it along the dashed line (figure 2).

figure 3

figure 1   figure 2

♦ Then they can fold the top edge of the paper downward and tuck it behind the folded strip, like a matchbook. They should crease the fold at the top (figure 3).

♦ Across the lower front strips of the three "matchbooks" instruct them to write *Past Tense*, *Present Tense*, and *Future Tense.*

♦ Now it is time for them to open up the panels and write their three paragraphs on the appropriate page—past, present, or future.

♦ Then they should close the matchbooks and draw a picture on the cover that conveys the main idea of the paragraph.

♦ Distribute one sheet of construction paper per student. Have students cut their sheet into a 7- by 14-inch rectangle. Have them glue their three paragraphs onto the construction paper as shown in figure 4.

♦ Hang their finished projects on a bulletin board under a banner that reads TOMORROW, TODAY WILL BE YESTERDAY.

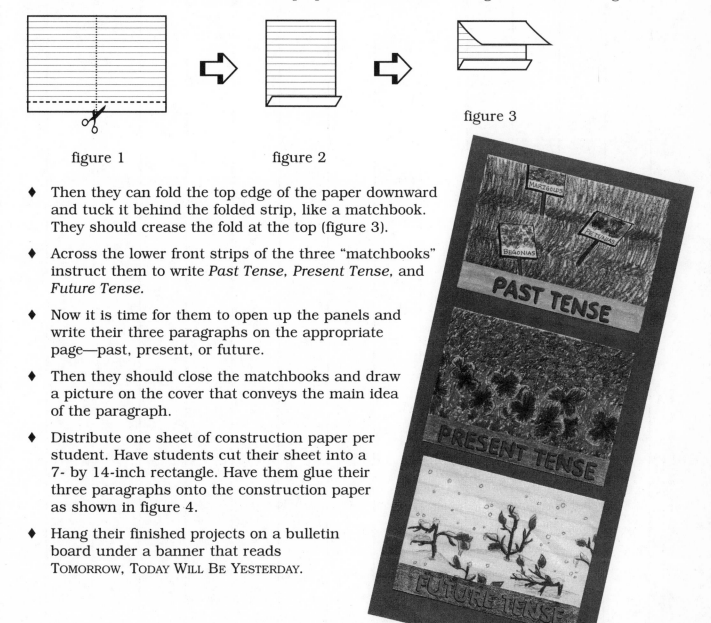

figure 4

Terrific, Specific Adjectives

Create a dazzling display of twirling ornament books for your classroom as students explore important story elements and descriptive adjectives.

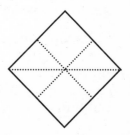

Materials

* 8½- by 11-inch copy paper
* scissors
* glue sticks
* one bead for each student with a hole large enough to hold doubled ribbon
* ribbon or yarn
* colored pencils
* oaktag

Creating the Bulletin Board

♦ Give each student three sheets of copy paper.

♦ Direct students to pull the top left corner of one sheet down diagonally to the right so that the top edge of the paper aligns with the right edge of the paper. Crease along the fold (figure 1).

♦ Then they can cut off the bottom strip of paper so that they are left with an 8½-inch square (figure 2).

♦ Students should fold the square in half vertically and crease it. Once they open it, they can then fold it in half horizontally and crease it again. When opened, the paper will have three creases (figure 3).

♦ Ask them to repeat these steps for all three pieces of copy paper.

♦ Have students place the paper in front of them so that the bottom corner is pointing at them (figure 4). There will be two diamonds and four triangles created by the folds.

♦ In the top diamond on page 1, students should draw a picture of the protagonist from a novel that they have read. In the two triangles to the left and right of this diamond, have them write a total of six adjectives which describe the protagonist. Encourage students to use a thesaurus to find the most fitting adjectives.

♦ In the bottom diamond on page 1, students should draw a picture of the main setting from the novel. In the two triangles to the left and right of this diamond, have them write a total of six adjectives which describe the setting (figure 5).

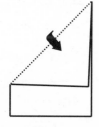

figure 1

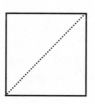

figure 2

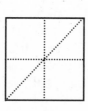

figure 3

figure 4

♦ In the top diamond on page 2, students should draw a picture of the antagonist from the novel. Have them write six adjectives that describe this person or thing in the triangles that frame the illustration.

♦ A picture of their favorite scene from the novel will go in the bottom diamond on page 2. The two triangles that frame this diamond will feature a pair of sentences that describe this scene, each sentence containing at least three descriptive adjectives. Students should underline the adjectives.

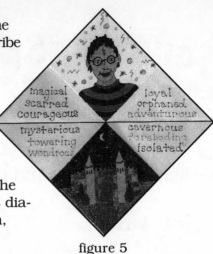

figure 5

♦ In the top diamond on page 3, students will draw a picture of the main problem from the novel. The two triangles that frame this diamond will feature a pair of sentences that describe the problem, each sentence containing at least three descriptive adjectives. Students should underline the adjectives.

♦ In the bottom diamond on page 3, students can draw a picture of the solution to the problem from the novel. In the two triangles that frame this diamond, they will write a pair of sentences that describe the solution, each sentence containing at least three descriptive adjectives. Students should underline the adjectives.

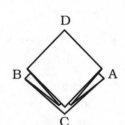

♦ Instruct students to use colored pencils to color the twelve triangular shapes on the sides opposite their writing.

♦ Then have them fold the paper in half along the diagonal crease so that the writing is on the inside (figure 6). They should push points A and B into the inside to point C, making a smaller square (figure 7). They can now do this to all three pages.

figure 6

♦ Ask students to glue the back of the bottom picture of page 1 to the back of the top picture of page 2, making sure to line up point D on both pages. Then they should glue the back of the bottom picture of page 2 to the back of the *bottom* picture of page 3, making sure to line up point D on both pages.

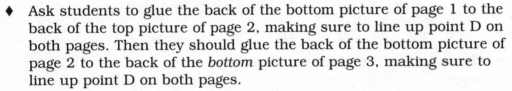

figure 7

♦ Have them glue a 36-inch ribbon around the stack of pages along the C–D line on both sides, leaving tails of equal lengths hanging from point C (figure 8).

♦ Students should cut two 4 ¼-inch squares from the card stock and glue one piece to each side of the stack of pages, covering the ribbons.

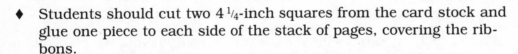

♦ Then they can thread both ends of the ribbon through the bead. Tie the ends of the ribbons with a couple of knots to prevent the bead from sliding off (figure 9).

figure 8

♦ To open the ornament book, slide the bead up to the knot and open the pages so that the covers meet. Slide the bead down to lock the book into place.

♦ To display the ornament books, hang a string across the classroom. Tie varying lengths of thread from the string. Tie a paper clip to the end of each piece of thread and hang the ornament books from the paper clips. When a breeze blows past the ornament books, they spin and create a dazzling display to jazz up the classroom.

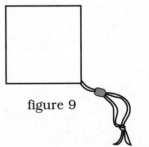

figure 9

Settings That Stand Out

What would the Harry Potter series be without Hogwarts?
What would Charlotte's Web be without the barnyard?
Vividly realized settings can make a story come alive for the reader.

Materials

* glue sticks or spray glue
* colored markers or pencils
* $8\frac{1}{2}$- by 11-inch copy paper
* thin black markers
* scissors
* oaktag

Creating the Bulletin Board

♦ Have students brainstorm a list of things that could be found in the main setting of a novel that they've read.

♦ On sheets of copy paper, students should draw pictures of the main characters and objects in that setting. Instruct them to think about things that might be seen in the foreground, midground, and background of the scene. They should first draw the scene in pencil, outline it with a black marker, and then erase the stray pencil marks. See example to the right. (In the three-dimensional, final version of this project, the objects marked with an "**B**" will appear in the midground; the objects marked with a "**B**" will appear in the foreground; the **A**'s and **B**'s will not appear in the final picture.)

♦ Make three copies of the picture that each student drew.

♦ Students should use glue sticks or spray glue to attach one of the copies to a sheet of oaktag. This will make the picture sturdier.

♦ Students will then color the picture using markers or colored pencils.

♦ On a copy of the picture, students should color the objects and characters that will appear in the midground and foreground of the picture.

♦ Tell students to cut out these items, glue them onto oaktag, and then cut them out again. If two or more of the objects overlap and appear in the same layer (such as the duck and rat in the picture on page 19), they should cut them out as a single piece.

♦ These items will be affixed to the main picture with small tabs so they will stand out. Have students cut out several dozen thin one-inch strips of oaktag.

♦ They will fold the small strips in half and then in half again, creating three creases with four small panels. Then they should tear off one of the small panels on the strips, leaving three panels (with two folds).

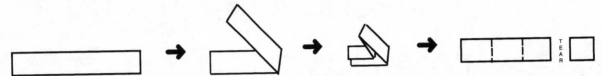

♦ Have students fold these tabs into brackets, put some glue on one end of each bracket, and affix it to the backs of the midground and foreground objects. Several brackets should be glued onto each object to give it support, varying the directions in which each of the brackets face.

front   back

♦ Students should put glue on the other end of the bracket and glue these objects onto the background picture so that they pop out.

♦ On the third copy of the picture, students will color the objects which will appear in the foreground, cut these objects out, glue them onto oaktag, and then cut them out again.

♦ Have them glue brackets to these objects. Then they should glue them onto the tops of their counterparts in the midground layer so they pop out into the foreground. The pictures will now have three layers—a background, a midground, and a foreground.

♦ Students will then glue the completed picture onto a large sheet of oaktag or poster board so that there is a two-inch border across the top, a one-inch border down the sides, and a six-inch writing area at the bottom.

♦ In the space above the picture they should use creative lettering to write the name of the novel the picture illustrates.

♦ In the writing area below the picture instruct them to write a complete, detailed paragraph which describes the setting and explains its importance to the story.

♦ Hang up the completed projects on a bulletin board. Add a banner that reads SETTINGS THAT STAND OUT. Curve the banner in and out a few times to give it a wavy, three-dimensional effect. Tape the banner to the bulletin board wherever the banner touches the bulletin board.

CHARLOTTE'S WEB

The farmyard is the major setting of Charlotte's Web. It is here where the "miracle" of the writing in the web occurs and where the animals gather to discuss Wilbur's fate. The scene occasionally shifts to Fern's house or to the county fair, but those are secondary settings. Even the ending of the story, when most of Charlotte's children float away on their web balloons, happens in the farmyard. This setting is where Wilbur finds happiness and where he will spend the rest of his life.

Writing Can Be Colorful!

Teach students to consider their word choices carefully to add the right touch of color to their writing.

Materials

* Peacock template (page 23)
* Feathers template (page 24)
* scissors
* colored pencils
* black marker

Creating the Bulletin Board

♦ Sometimes students will use words in their writing which are dull and lifeless, or they may use the same words over and over again. This bulletin board will help them find more colorful words to express themselves in their writing.

♦ Copy and cut out one peacock and as many feathers as you wish.

♦ Color the peacock. Then use a marker to write an overused or dull word on the peacock's sign (for example, *walk*).

♦ Tape the peacock onto a bulletin board. Add a banner that reads WRITING CAN BE COLORFUL!

♦ Distribute the feathers, and randomly select students to give more interesting synonyms for the featured word (such as *amble, limp, plod*). Each student should write a word on one of the feathers, color it, and tape it behind the peacock on the bulletin board. As more words are added, the peacock's tail will grow larger and more colorful.

♦ Leave this peacock up for one or two weeks. Each day during the first minute of language class, invite students to add new word feathers to the peacock.

♦ Repeat this activity every week or two. After a while, students will naturally learn to expand their word choices to make their writing more colorful and lively.

♦ Consider having the students work in cooperative groups to create a larger bulletin board which features several peacocks. Each group can be given a peacock which features a different word. The bulletin board can be titled MUSTERING UP SOME COLORFUL WORDS, because a group of peacocks is called a muster.

♦ Suggested words to use: walk, said, ate, big, asked, happy, sad, nice, pretty, like, saw, small, think, home, fast.

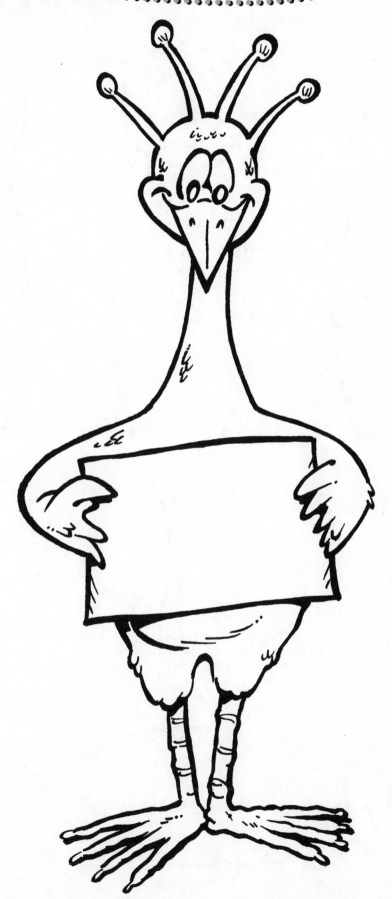

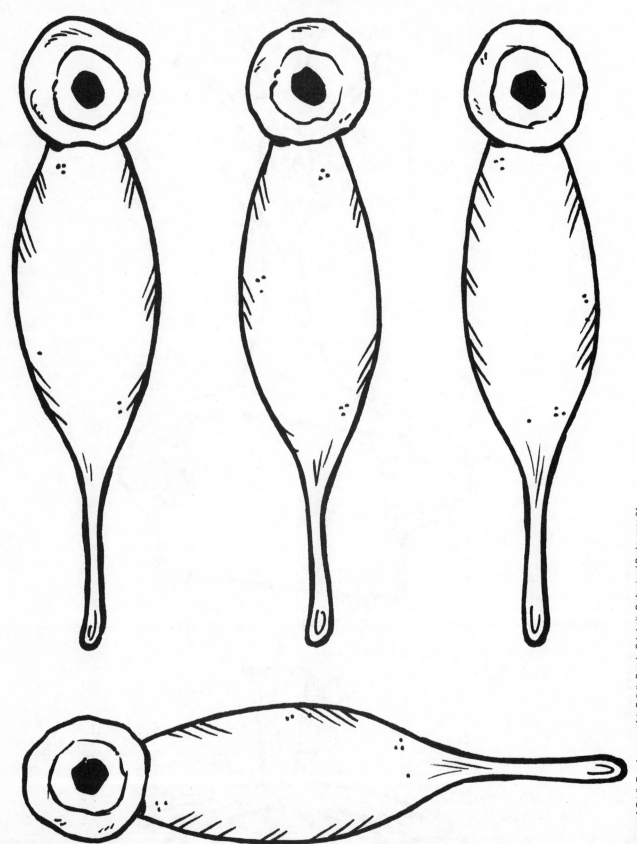

You Don't Say!

Laughter is the best medicine . . . for turning an ordinary vocabulary lesson into one that students are sure to remember.

Materials

* scissors
* strips of paper
* colored pencils
* large can
* Flapbook templates copied back to back (pages 26 and 27)

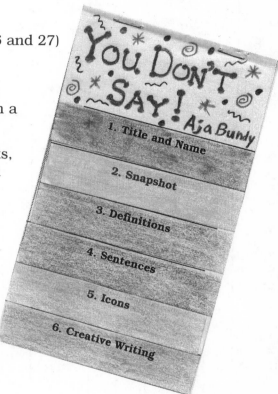

Playing the Game

♦ Write each of your vocabulary or spelling words on a strip of paper, and put them into a can or hat.

♦ Divide the class into groups of four or five students, and have each group pick five random words from the can.

♦ Give the groups about five minutes to create two-minute scenes that use all five of their words. The words should be used in context, so that their meanings can be understood. Groups can use a dictionary if they are unsure of a word's meaning. They should discuss a basic outline for the scene and then improvise during the performance. Tell students to spread the words out during the scene and to not have the same person say all of the words.

Creating the Bulletin Board

♦ Make two-sided copies of the Flapbook templates. Panel 6 should be inverted on the back of panel 1. Hold on to them until after you conduct the activity above.

♦ After the groups have performed their scenes, pass out the Flapbook template. Have students cut along the dotted lines to create three panels from the page (figure 1).

♦ Have them place the panels on top of each other, so that panels 1, 2, and 3 show (figure 2).

♦ Then they should bend the tops of the panels backward so that they wrap around and reveal panels 4, 5, and 6. Fasten the top with two staples (figure 3).

♦ Students can then follow the directions on each of the panels to complete the flapbook.

♦ Hang the flapbooks on a bulletin board under a banner that reads YOU DON'T SAY!

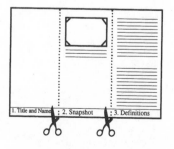

figure 1

figure 2

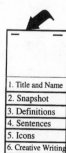

figure 3

Draw a simple icon in each box to help you remember the meaning of each word. Write the word on the line at the top of the box.

1.

2.

3.

4.

5.

3. Definitions

Write a paragraph describing the plot of the scene your group performed.

2. Snapshot

1. Title and Name

Use each word in a sentence
in a way that conveys its meaning.

1.

2.

3.

4.

5.

4. Sentences

Write the five words and their definitions.

1.

2.

3.

4.

5.

5. Icons

Draw a picture of yourself
performing in your scene.

6. Creative Writing

Words for the Wise

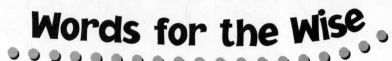

Creating "Word Wheels" challenges students to explore the deeper meanings of their vocabulary or spelling words.

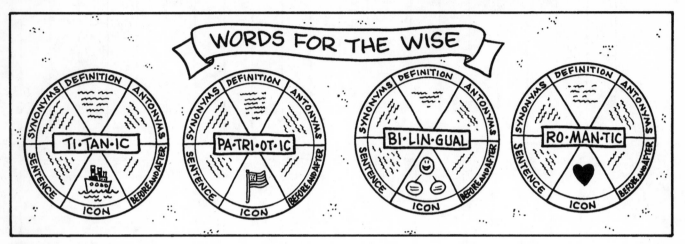

aterials

✳ colored pencils   ✳ scissors   ✳ Word Wheel template (page 29)

Creating the Bulletin Board

♦ Give each student a copy of the Word Wheel template.

♦ Assign a different spelling or vocabulary word to each student. Students will study their words in more depth as they complete the word wheel.

♦ Review the following directions with your students so they understand how to complete the word wheel:

   ♦ Break the word down into syllables and write it in the box in the center of the circle (i.e., syl • la • bles).

   ♦ In the DEFINITION wedge, write the dictionary definition of the word.

   ♦ Use a thesaurus to find as many synonyms and antonyms of the word as you can. Write them in the SYNONYMS and ANTONYMS wedges of the circle.

   ♦ In the ICON wedge, draw a simple icon that conveys the meaning of the word. The icon can be a simple symbol in the style of a road sign. (Students will have to be creative if the word is not a noun.)

   ♦ In the SENTENCE wedge, write a complete sentence using the word in a way that conveys its meaning.

   ♦ Find the word in the dictionary. In the BEFORE AND AFTER wedge, write each word that comes immediately before and immediately after the word.

♦ Students should cut out the wheels. Hang the word wheels on a bulletin board under a banner that reads WORDS FOR THE WISE.

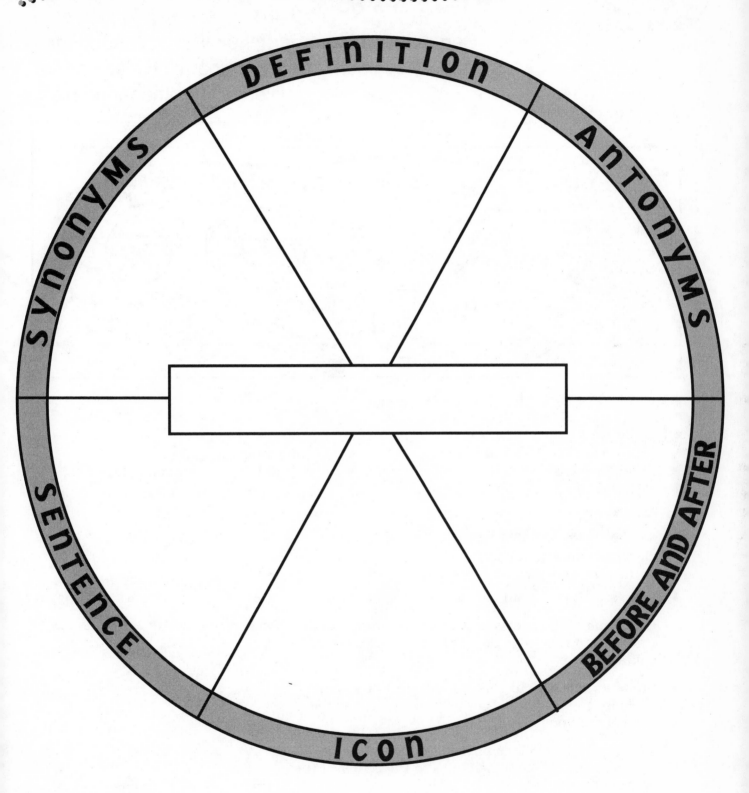

DEFINITION

SYNONYMS

ANTONYMS

SENTENCE

BEFORE AND AFTER

ICON

Homophone Pie

Serve students a hearty helping of homophones
as they cook up an imaginative bulletin board
filled with homophone pies.

Materials

* glue sticks
* colored pencils
* scissors
* oaktag
* tape
* Writing template (page 32)
* Milk and Utensils template (page 33)

Creating the Bulletin Board

♦ Give each student a sheet of oaktag and two copies
of the Writing template.

♦ Have students cut out the two circles.

♦ Using one of the circles as a template, they should
trace around the edge of the circle onto a piece of
oaktag.

♦ Students can cut out this oaktag circle and set it
aside for the moment. They will use it later as the
base of the homophone pie.

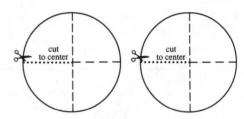

figure 1

♦ On both of the circle templates, students should
cut along one of the dotted lines to the center of the
circles (figure 1).

♦ Starting at the slit and going clockwise, students
should use a pencil to lightly number the sections
of one circle 1, 2, 3, 4. They should number the
other circle 5, 6, 7, 8 (figure 2).

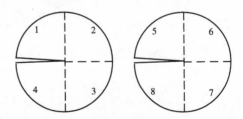

figure 2

◆ Students should lay the circle numbered 5–8 on top of the circle numbered 1–4, with the slits aligned. Have them tape together the edges of sections 4 and 5 as shown. To make this easier, they can fold section 8 out of the way.

◆ Students should fold section 8 on top of section 7. Then they will fold these two sections on top of section 6, and so forth until they have a book shaped like a pie wedge.

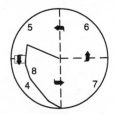

◆ Have students open up the top flap of the book. On section 1 they should write a complete sentence which contains a pair of homophones, such as, *The maid at the lodge made our beds every day before we returned from skiing.* On the other section (which is actually the reverse side of section 3) students can draw a picture illustrating the sentence they wrote. (This idea can also be used for homographs or homonyms.)

◆ Then, students will open up the book to the next pair of panels. In section 2 they will write another sentence that contains a pair of homophones, and they will

illustrate the sentence on the other section. They should continue doing this until they have written and illustrated seven sentences.

◆ After they have finished the interior of the pie book, they should refold it. Tell them to put glue on the back of panel 2 and glue it onto the oaktag circle as shown.

◆ They should write the words "Homophone Pie" on the oaktag and decorate it so it looks like a pie crust. Make sure they write their name somewhere on the pie.

◆ Have students decorate the cover of the pie book so that it looks like a slice of pie has been cut away.

◆ Hang all the pie "plates" on a bulletin board. Create a banner that reads HAVE A SLICE OF HOMOPHONE PIE! Cut out and color the milk and utensils from the template and add them to the bulletin board.

Homophone Pie Writing template

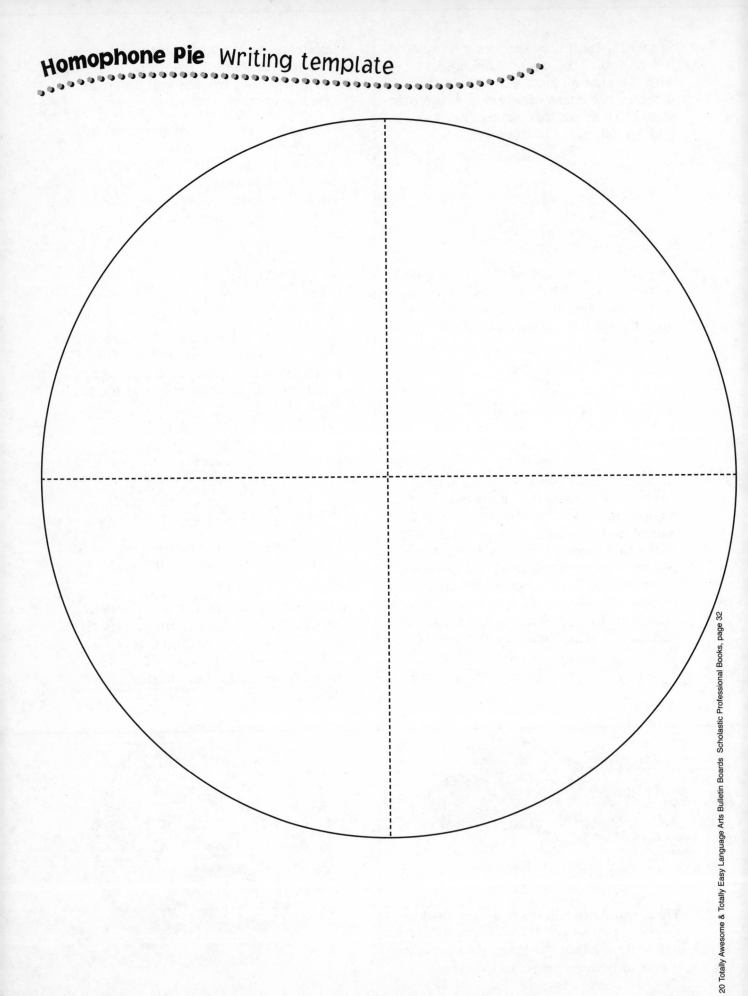

Sentences Don't Bug Us!

After playing a fun Language Arts game, students will create a whimsical, colorful bulletin board.

Materials

* scissors   * glue sticks   * liquid glue   * 12-inch pipe cleaners
* Sentence Switch-a-Roo sheet (page 36)
* Bug template (page 37) copied onto four different colors of paper

Playing the Game

♦ Give each student a copy of the Sentence Switch-a-Roo sheet.

♦ Divide the class into groups of four. Have each group sit in a circle. (They can be seated around a table, or they can push their desks into a small cluster.)

♦ Each student in the group should write a declarative sentence on the top line of the Sentence Switch-a-Roo sheet. (i.e., *My brother Keith saw a killer whale when he went sailing.*)

♦ Next, instruct students to pass the papers clockwise and silently read the sentences their classmates wrote. On the second line, they will change these sentences into interrogative ones. (i.e., *Did Keith see a killer whale when he went sailing?*)

♦ Have them switch papers a second time and change the sentences to imperative ones. (i.e., *Keith, look at the killer whale.*)

♦ They should then switch the papers a third time and change the sentences to exclamatory ones. (i.e., *Wow, I can't believe Keith saw a killer whale when he went sailing!*)

♦ Finally, tell them to pass the papers back to the original writer. Each student should read the variations of their original sentence and make sure they were done properly. If there are any questions, you can review with that group.

♦ Have the students repeat this activity in the two other writing areas on the Sentence Switch-a-Roo sheet.

♦ After the game students will review the three sets of sentences and choose the foursome they like best. They can adjust or reword any of the sentences if they desire.

♦ Give each student two different colors of the Bug template. Students should cut each page in half along the dotted line and exchange the circles with their classmates so that everyone has four circles of different colors.

♦ On the lines at the top of each of the circles, have them write one of the four sentences that they chose. Each circle will feature a different type of sentence (figure 1).

♦ In the lower left-hand quadrant, they will describe the type of sentence featured on the lines at the top. They can use the descriptions of the four sentences that can be found at the top of the Sentence Switch-a-Roo sheet. This information should be written diagonally within the lower left-hand quadrant (figure 1).

♦ After they've written the information, have them cut out the four circles.

♦ Students will fold the circle horizontally and then vertically along the central lines. It is easier to fold along these lines if the circles are folded with the writing side facing out.

♦ Then they should open the circles and cut along the dotted line, up to the centerpoint (figure 1).

♦ Have them use a glue stick to glue the lower right-hand panel behind the lower left-hand panel on each of the circles. This will make the top two panels stand vertically (figure 2).

♦ They will then glue the vertical panels of the four shapes back-to-back so they form a dome (figure 3). This will be the body of a bug.

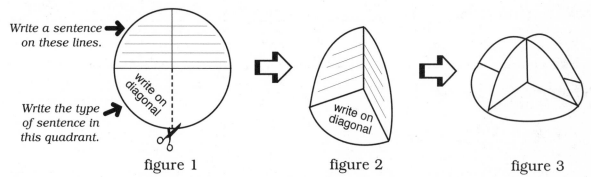

Write a sentence on these lines.

write on diagonal

Write the type of sentence in this quadrant.

figure 1   figure 2   figure 3

♦ Give each student three 12-inch pipe cleaners. Have them lay these down in an asterisk pattern and then glue them to the bottom of the dome. These will form the bug's legs. Students can bend the pipe cleaners to form joints.

♦ Students should cut out the bug's head from the template and glue the "neck" to the underside of the bug's body. (They can add a curly tongue to the bug if they'd like.)

♦ Staple a couple of the bug's feet to the bulletin board so they are secure. Make it look like the bugs are scurrying across the board. Add a banner that reads SENTENCES DON'T BUG US!

♦ With a little creativity you can use this dome-shape in other ways. Make the dome-shape the stomach of a teddy bear; put three dome-shapes together to form snowmen; or turn them into a display that looks like a balloon bouquet.

Sentence Switch-a-Roo Sheet

NAME: _____

> A **declarative sentence** makes a statement and ends with a period.
>
> An **interrogative sentence** asks a question and ends with a question mark.
>
> An **imperative sentence** gives a command and ends with a period.
>
> An **exclamatory sentence** expresses excitement and ends with an exclamation point.

Declarative   1. _____
_____

Interrogative   2. _____
_____

Imperative   3. _____
_____

Exclamatory   4. _____
_____

Interrogative   1. _____
_____

Exclamatory   2. _____
_____

Declarative   3. _____
_____

Imperative   4. _____
_____

Imperative   1. _____
_____

Declarative   2. _____
_____

Exclamatory   3. _____
_____

Interrogative   4. _____
_____

Sentences Don't Bug Us!

Bug template

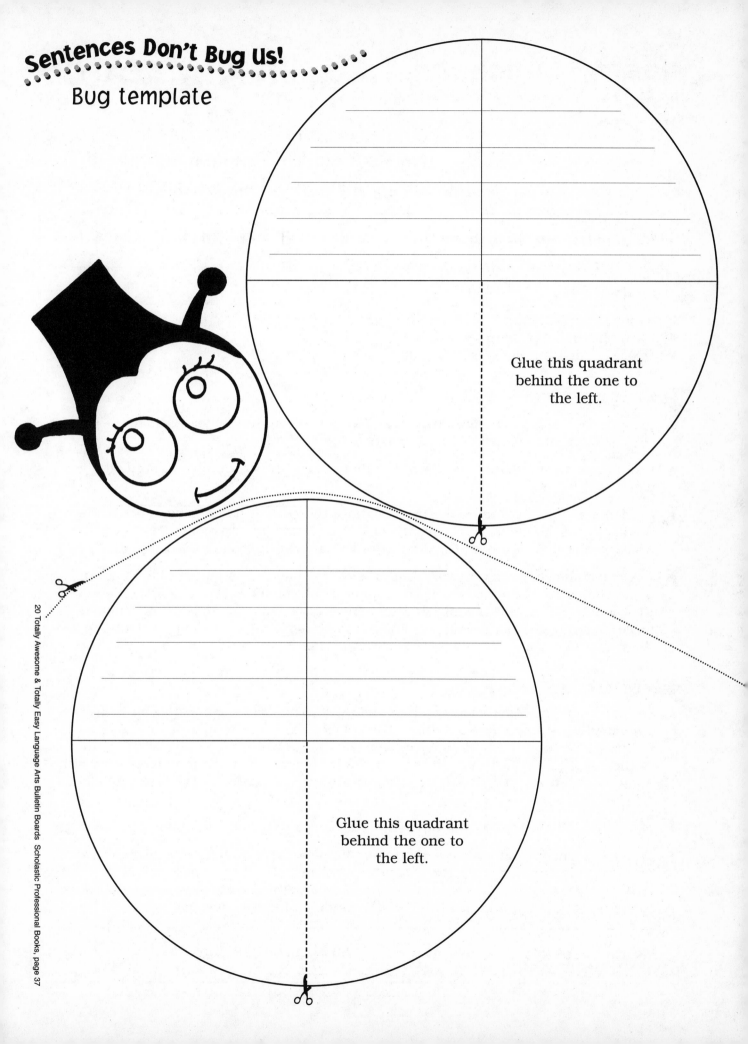

Glue this quadrant
behind the one to
the left.

Glue this quadrant
behind the one to
the left.

It's a Match!

Who says Language Arts has to be boring?
Here's a fun-filled game that's sure to have
students laughing about subjects and predicates.

| Mr. Gravois, our English teacher, | drools down his chin at breakfast. |

Materials

* Sentence strips and ribbon (pages 39 and 40)
* It's a Match! template (page 41)
* colored pencils or markers

Playing the Game

♦ Cut out each of the sentence strips. Each strip will contain half of a sentence—either the complete subject half or the complete predicate half.

♦ Hand them out randomly to students. If there is an uneven number of students, you can join the game.

♦ Students should determine whether they have the subject half of a sentence or the predicate half. Students who have the subjects should line up along one wall of the classroom. Those who have the predicates will line up opposite the first group.

♦ Ask one of the students with a subject to select a student with a predicate. Both students should step into the center. The complete subject should be read first, followed by the complete predicate. The mixed-up sentences are a sure way to generate laughter while exploring a rather dry subject. (As the game is played, if a student is found to be on the wrong side, you know his understanding of this concept needs further exploration.)

Creating the Bulletin Board

♦ On the It's a Match! template, each student will write the sentence that his or her combined subject/predicate created. The subject should be written in one color and the predicate in another. Then have each student draw a zany picture of the sentence in the snapshot area. Attach an IT'S A MATCH ribbon to any of the templates where the subjects and predicates match up to make the original sentence. (The ribbon is found on page 40.)

♦ Hang their finished work on a bulletin board under a banner that reads IT'S A MATCH!

♦ When you learn about simple subjects and predicates, play this game again, except after the zany sentences are read have the student holding the complete subject identify the simple subject. The other student should identify the simple predicate. This is a fun, easy way to evaluate students' understanding of these concepts.

| My two-week-old baby brother | howls loudly at the moon every night. |

The 100-foot-tall gorilla with razor sharp teeth

sent people running down the street in a panic.

My two-week-old baby brother

drools down his chin at breakfast.

, our language arts teacher,

(Write teacher's name here.)

is one of the best teachers I've ever had!

The amazing magician in the long black cape

makes a woman disappear before your very eyes.

The fearless paratrooper in the blue skydiving uniform

jumps out of airplanes for fun.

A ferocious lion in the African desert

caught the zebra with one swipe of his claw.

The funny clown with the bright red cheeks

wears a curly, green wig and oversized pants.

The clumsy scientist who works in the lab

accidentally triggered an explosion.

The graceful giraffe with the brown spots

has a fifteen-foot-long neck.

, a really nice classmate of mine,

(Write a student's name here.)

stayed up all night to study for an English test.

A black cat that lives in the alley behind my house

howls loudly at the moon every night.

The disoriented sea captain

got marooned on a desert island.

It's a Match!

NAME: _____

SUBJECT:
_____

_____

PREDICATE:
_____

_____

Paragraph Sandwiches

Like a good sandwich, a paragraph needs
some "meat" to give it substance.

Materials

* Sandwich template (page 43)
* colored pencils
* scissors

Getting Started

♦ Review the basic rules for writing paragraphs. Remind students of the elements of a
good paragraph: topic sentence, detail sentences, and concluding sentence.

♦ Compare writing a paragraph to making a sandwich, the bread representing the sentences that frame the paragraph, and the meat, lettuce, and tomato representing the
substance and details of the paragraph.

Creating the Bulletin Board

♦ Pass out a copy of the Sandwich template to each student.

♦ Assign a topic for students to write about.

♦ Have them write a topic sentence on the upper bun, several detail sentences on the
condiment and meat layers, and a concluding sentence on the bottom bun.

♦ Students should cut out the sandwiches and color them.

♦ Hang them on a bulletin board under a banner that reads PARAGRAPH SANDWICHES.

You've Got Mail!

In-class correspondence becomes as simple as dropping a letter in a mailbox with this interactive bulletin board.

Materials

* Mailbox template (page 46)
* manila folders
* glue sticks
* brass fasteners
* scissors
* colored pencils

Creating the Bulletin Board

♦ Give each student a manila folder and a copy of the Mailbox template. Have students cut out the mailbox and the flag.

♦ They can then color the mailbox and flag, and write their name in creative letters in the rectangle on the side of the mailbox.

♦ They should glue the mailbox onto the manila folder so that the bottom of the mailbox aligns along the folded edge.

♦ Have them cut out the mailbox, making sure that they are cutting both sides of the manila folder. When they are done, they will have a folder in the shape of a mailbox.

♦ Instruct them to glue the flag onto some of the manila folder scraps and cut it out.

♦ They should place the flag on top of the mailbox so the two black dots align and then push a brass fastener through the black dots. Only the top panel of the manila folder should be fastened to the flag. The flag can now be lifted and lowered to indicate whether or not there is mail in the box.

♦ Have them cut out the mail slot on the left side of the mailbox. Only the top panel of the manila folder should be cut during this step.

♦ Then they should glue the top and side edges of the manila mailbox closed. Letters can now be inserted into the slot without falling out.

♦ Hang a banner on the bulletin board that reads YOU'VE GOT MAIL! Under the banner add the mailboxes. You might want to have students make "wooden" posts out of construction paper for the mailboxes to sit on.

Using the Bulletin Board

♦ This bulletin board can be used for a variety of Language Arts activities.

Mail Center—Students could use the mailboxes to send notes, cards, Valentines, and letters to classmates. You might want to write occasional notes to students who don't receive mail from classmates.

Back to School Night—Students could write a letter discussing their goals for the coming school year. They could address it to their parents and put it in their mailbox. On *Back to School Night*, the parents could get the letter from their child's mailbox, read it, and write a response for their child to pick up the next day.

Language Arts—As students learn how to write "friendly letters" and "business letters," they could put the finished letters in their mailboxes for you to collect and grade.

First Week of School—Students could write postcards to the class as if they were written from the previous summer and which feature an activity they did or a trip they took. The postcard could include a related drawing and paragraph which the students could share with the class. The postcards could then be placed in their mailboxes.

Class Jobs—Each mailbox could feature the name of a class job on its side. Envelopes with students' names along the edge could be placed into the mailbox, showing which student is responsible for each of the jobs that week.

Attendance and Lunch Count—In addition to the mailboxes, the bulletin board should feature two large mail sacks which have numerous slits out of which letters can stick. One sack should have the word "School" on the side, and the other should have the word "Home" on the side. The mail sacks indicate where the student will eat lunch that day—home or school. (Or you could have them indicate whether the student is buying lunch or bringing their own lunch.)

In the morning, every mailbox will have an envelope sticking out with a student's name written on it. As the students arrive, they could take their letter out of the mailbox and put it into the appropriate mail sack. This makes it easy to take lunch count without disrupting the students' morning work. Any letter left in a mailbox means that student is absent.

When the students return from lunch they should put their letters back in their mailboxes so the bulletin board is ready for the next day.

Try It! You'll Like It!

Students will form mini ad agencies—complete with copywriters and art editors—as they create a product, develop a marketing plan, and hone their powers of persuasion.

Materials

* old magazines
* Requirement sheet (page 49)
* 8½- by 11-inch copy paper
* 1 sheet of bulletin board paper (approximately 3 feet by 4 feet) for each group
* tape recorder, blank tapes, and video camera (optional)

* scissors
* colored pencils
* construction paper

Getting Started

♦ Have students look at ads in old magazines. Ask them to find examples of ways advertisers try to entice the reader into buying their product.

♦ Review the following propaganda techniques found in advertising. Ask students to find examples of these techniques in the magazine ads.

Bandwagon Technique—persuading people to buy a product by letting them know that other people are buying it

Testimonials/Transfer—using the words (testimonial) or images (transfer) of famous people to persuade you to buy the product

Association—associating the product with fun times, patriotism, relaxation, or the like

Glittering Generalities—using exaggerated, flowery words to describe a product

Repetition—repeating the product's name at least four times to make you remember it

Bait and Switch—baiting consumers with a "FREE" offer, only to find out in the small print that they actually need four box tops, plus postage and handling.

♦ Divide students into groups of four or five. Each group should brainstorm types of products for which they could design an ad campaign. Have them choose the product from their list that most excites them.

♦ Then they should decide what the *target audience* is for their product and discuss information about the product that they feel should be mentioned in their advertising.

♦ Review the Requirement sheet with the class.

> ♦ To help with the television commercial part of this project, you might want to show examples of storyboards to your class. There are many examples on the Internet that you can find by typing "storyboard" into a search engine.

> ♦ Consider having the students act out the radio and television ads for the class. You might want them to record the radio spots and television commercials. The class would enjoy hearing and watching themselves.

♦ It will be up to each group to decide which member(s) will be responsible for completing each element. Students can select jobs based on their talents. Copywriters can write the copy for the ads and for the press release. Art directors can design the logo and visual components of the ads. Traffic managers can organize the workers so that everything is being completed in a timely fashion.

♦ Students must share responsibility for completing the poster. Tell them that part of their final grade will be determined by how well they share in the production of the poster. If someone finishes his or her section of the poster, he or she should help the other members. Remind them that each member of the group is responsible for proofreading *each* element of their project.

♦ Have the groups present their products to the class, reviewing and discussing each element of the project.

♦ After the oral presentations, groups should glue the print ad, the storyboard, the radio script, the press release, and the logo and tag line to the poster. Have them attach the packaging to the poster in such a way that it allows all sides of the package to be seen. For example, they could tie a string to the package and tape the string to the poster, allowing the package to hang freely.

♦ Hang the posters in the hall or on a class wall for everyone to see. Add a large banner that reads TRY IT! YOU'LL LIKE IT!

TITLE

♦ Write the title TRY IT! YOU'LL LIKE IT! across the top of your poster and list the complete name of each group member.

PRODUCT

♦ Create a package for your product. You can cover a box with construction paper and write the product's information on it.

♦ Add the title PRODUCT and attach the package to your poster. You could tie a string to the package and tape the string to the poster, allowing the package to hang freely.

PRODUCT IDENTIFICATION

♦ Design a logo for your product. Draw it on a sheet of construction paper.

♦ Write a tag line for your product. Write it creatively on a strip of construction paper.

♦ Add the title PRODUCT IDENTIFICATION and attach the logo and tag line to your poster.

PRINT AD

♦ Design a magazine print ad for your product on a piece of paper that measures at least $8\frac{1}{2}$ by 11 inches. Use one of the propaganda techniques discussed in class to help sell your product. Look at other magazine ads to get ideas.

♦ Add the title PRINT AD and attach the advertisement to your poster.

TELEVISION COMMERCIAL

♦ Write a television commercial for your product that includes a different propaganda technique from the one used in the print ad.

♦ Create a storyboard for your commercial that shows the different camera angles used as well as the dialogue spoken by the actors or narrators. Each panel should be at least 5 inches square.

♦ Add the title TELEVISION COMMERCIAL and attach the storyboard to your poster.

RADIO SPOT

♦ Write the script for a 30–45 second radio commercial that includes a different propaganda technique from the ones used in the print ad or the television commercial.

♦ The script should include all the dialogue spoken by the actors and narrators. Note where music or sound effects are supposed to occur.

♦ Add the title RADIO SPOT and attach the script to your poster.

PRESS RELEASE

♦ Write a press release for your product that announces its introduction to the public. The press release should contain a different propaganda technique from those already used.

♦ Add the title PRESS RELEASE and attach the press release to your poster.

Figuratively Speaking

Figurative language is like a blossom on a rose bush. It can help an otherwise dull sentence sparkle with color and life.

Materials

* tape
* colored pencils
* construction paper
* glue sticks or spray glue
* Figures of Speech list (page 52)
* Figures of Speech template (page 53)
* white legal paper (8½ by 14 inches)

Getting Started

♦ Discuss the meanings of the figures of speech with the class and show them the examples on page 52.

♦ Students should pick a subject for which they will write a seven sentence paragraph. Each sentence will feature a different figure of speech. First have students write a rough draft on a lined sheet of paper.

Creating the Bulletin Board

♦ Pass out a copy of the Figures of Speech list and template to each student. Students will write the final version of their paragraph on the template. Each sentence should be written in a different color.

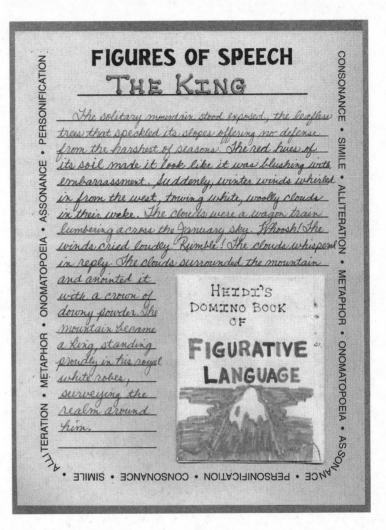

♦ Have students use glue sticks or spray glue to attach the template to a sheet of colored construction paper to give it a more finished look.

♦ Then distribute sheets of white legal paper, which students will use to construct a domino book.

♦ First students should cut the sheet in half vertically so they end up with two long strips of paper.

♦ Next have them place the strips next to each other horizontally as shown and tape the edges, forming one long strip.

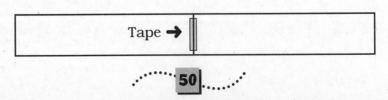

Tape →

- Then they will fold this long strip in half three times. When they open it back up, the strip will be divided into eight panels, as shown below.

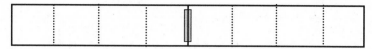

- Tell them to fold the far right edge inward, creasing the paper along the first fold.

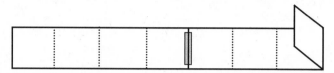

- They will continue to fold the paper inward (a total of seven times), creasing along each fold. When they have finished the last fold, students should flip the domino book over. The top panel will serve as the cover. (This panel should open toward the left, like the cover of a book. The interior panels will "roll" out toward the right.) On the cover, students should create a title, such as "Heidi's Domino Book of Figurative Language." They should also draw a picture that represents the main idea of their paragraph.

- When students open the cover, it will reveal two panels.

  - On the left panel ask them to use creative lettering to write the figure of speech featured in the first sentence of their paragraph. They should write it in the same color in which they wrote the first sentence. Have them write the definition of this term underneath it.

  - At the top of the right panel, using the same color pencil, students should write the first sentence from their paragraph. Underneath this sentence ask them to draw a simple picture that illustrates the main idea of the sentence.

- Have students open the domino book to the next two panels. On the left they will write the figure of speech from the second sentence (in the appropriate color) and its definition. On the right they will write the second sentence and draw a related picture.

- They should continue doing this until all seven figures of speech have been illustrated. (The photo below shows a domino book opened to reveal the third panel, which describes and illustrates the term "alliteration.")

- After students finish the domino book, have them glue it into the square in the lower right corner of the Figures of Speech template. (Students should put the glue onto the back of panel 2.)

- Create a banner for your bulletin board that reads FIGURATIVELY SPEAKING, and hang students' work around it.

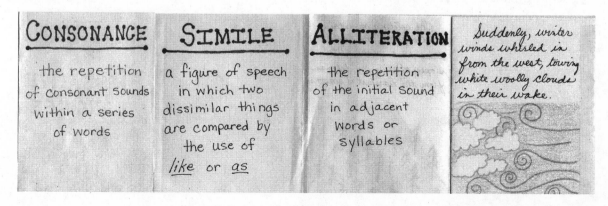

NAME: _____

CONSONANCE

the repetition of consonant sounds within a series of words

> **Example:** The solitary mountain stood exposed, the leafless trees that speckled its slopes offering no defense from the severest of seasons.

SIMILE

a figure of speech in which two dissimilar things are compared by the use of <u>like</u> or <u>as</u>

> **Example:** The red hues of its soil made it look like it was blushing with embarrassment.

ALLITERATION

the repetition of the initial sound in adjacent words or syllables

> **Example:** Suddenly, winter winds whirled in from the west, towing white, woolly clouds in their wake.

METAPHOR

a figure of speech in which two dissimilar things are compared without using the words <u>like</u> or <u>as</u>

> **Example:** The clouds were a wagon train lumbering across the January sky.

ONOMATOPOEIA

the use of a word whose spoken sound suggests the actual sound

> **Example:** Whoosh! The winds cried loudly. Rumble! The clouds whispered in reply.

ASSONANCE

the repetition of vowel sounds within a series of words

> **Example:** The clouds surrounded the mountain and anointed it with a crown of downy powder.

PERSONIFICATION

to show something that is not human behaving in a human or lifelike way

> **Example:** The mountain became king, standing proudly in his royal white robes, surveying the realm around him.

20 Totally Awesome & Totally Easy Language Arts Bulletin Boards Scholastic Professional Books, page 52

FIGURES OF SPEECH

_____

_____

_____

_____

_____

_____

_____

_____

_____

_____

_____

_____

_____

_____

_____

_____

Glue your domino book here.

CONSONANCE • SIMILE • ALLITERATION • METAPHOR • ONOMATOPOEIA • ASSONANCE

PERSONIFICATION • ASSONANCE • ONOMATOPOEIA • METAPHOR • ALLITERATION

• SIMILE • CONSONANCE • PERSONIFICATION •

Picture This

Explore concepts of imagery and meaning
by having students write poems
in descriptive shapes that reflect their theme.

Materials

* 8½- by 11-inch copy paper
* writing materials
* construction paper
* colored markers or pencils
* glue sticks or spray glue

Creating the Bulletin Board

* Show students examples of poems
  written in descriptive shapes—
  a poem about a garden in the
  shape of a flower, a poem about the
  sky in the form of a cloud, or a
  poem about a train ride in the shape
  of an engine.

* Ask the class leading questions:
  *Why might an author use this for-
  mat? Does it add to the imagery of
  the poem?*

* As a class, brainstorm a list of
  subjects that could be used for this
  kind of poetry.

* Have students write their own poem
  in this style. As a prompt, ask them
  to think of imagery related to their
  subject: *What might your subject feel, see, taste, hear, or smell? What might the subject
  sound like? Look like?
  Smell like? Feel like?*

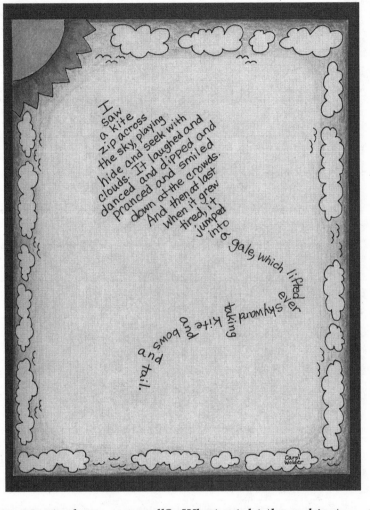

* Students should create a piece of stationery that features a border of related objects.
  For example, a poem in the shape of a skyscraper could have a border of buildings or
  cars; a poem in the shape of a bird might have a border of nests or eggs.

* They can write their typographical poem on the stationery using pencil in case they
  make a mistake. Then they should trace over the pencil with a marker.

* Have students glue their stationery onto a sheet of colored construction paper, leaving
  a colorful border around it.

* Hang the poems on a bulletin board under a banner that reads PICTURE THIS.

A Picture Is Worth 17 Syllables

Students will unlock their creativity by diving into this rapid-fire, free association writing activity.

Materials

* art paper
* construction paper
* 8½- by 11-inch copy paper
* colored markers or pencils
* photos from magazines and calendars, numbered
* glue sticks or spray glue

Getting Started

♦ Gather a collection of interesting photographs from magazines and calendars. Glue them onto pieces of oaktag for durability. Write a different number on each picture so they can be easily identified.

♦ Review the format of Haiku poetry with your students. Haikus are comprised of a five-syllable line, followed by a seven-syllable line, followed by a five-syllable line. Share some examples with them.

Creating the Bulletin Board

♦ Give each student a picture. Students should write the number of the picture as the title of their poem and then write a haiku poem that is inspired by that picture. Tell them to think of vivid adjectives that could describe the picture as they write their poems.

♦ As soon as students have written a haiku poem they should raise the picture in the air. Exchange that picture for a different one in your stack. Continue doing this for a period of 20–30 minutes. Each student will have several haiku poems written by the end of this time period.

♦ Students can then choose the haiku poem with which they are most pleased and work on refining it.

♦ They should write it neatly on a piece of art paper, add a decorative border to the poem, write their name on it, and glue it to a sheet of construction paper, leaving a one-inch border around it.

♦ Ask them to write the picture number on the back of the poem.

♦ Collect the poems. Hang the pictures on a bulletin board, and hang the haikus that are written about them around the corresponding pictures. Add a banner that reads A PICTURE IS WORTH SEVENTEEN SYLLABLES.

I'm a Poet, and I Know It

Students will be amazed at how poetic their writing can be when they just put their minds—and their five senses—to it.

Materials

* paper   * colored pencils and markers   * construction paper   * spray glue

Creating the Bulletin Board

STORMWASHED

The angry waves pounce on the shore,
    raking the sand with their claws.
The battered palm trees, roots exposed,
    bow in humble submission.

The absent seagulls, long since vanished,
    have silenced their crying caws.
The thunderful wind and drumming shower
    are locked in fierce competition.

The blanket of rain covers my body —
    retreats, advances, withdraws.
The stinging sand assaults my skin
    like pin-prick ammunition.

I stand. I drink rain. I pause.
I crouch. I lick my salty lips. I shift position.

I walk. I inhale Nature's cleansed soul.
    I veer and yaw.
I dance to the scent of lightning in anticipation
    of Nature's musician.

I am exhilarated.

♦ Turn off the lights, and have students close their eyes. Ask them to visualize themselves being somewhere else—an amusement park, a beach, a ski slope, a zoo—anywhere they'd like. After a few moments, ask them to visualize the things they would see there. Give them a minute to "see" things. Then ask them to envision what they would hear, taste, touch, and smell, again giving them time to visualize each of the senses.

♦ Turn on the lights and have students write two sentences, each beginning with "I see." Then for each sentence they should write something they would see at the place they imagined. (i.e., *I see waves. I see palm trees*.)

♦ Then they should write two sentences beginning with "I hear." (i.e., *I hear seagulls. I hear the wind*.)

♦ They should write two sentences for each of the other senses—I touch, I taste, and I smell.

♦ Have students write a final sentence beginning with "I feel," which describes how they would feel being at the place they visualized. This is their eleventh sentence.

♦ Then ask them to go back over their poem and draw a line through every "I see," "I hear," "I taste," etc. (i.e., leaving them with *Waves. Palm trees. Seagulls. Wind*.)

♦ Students should add adjectives and adverbs to the remaining phrases to make them more vibrant and clear. (i.e., *Angry, storm-tossed waves. Battered palm trees*.)

♦ Then have students scan their poems to find places where they could add similes, metaphors, and personification.

♦ Have students review the poems for word choices which could improve alliteration and assonance.

♦ When they are done, they should copy their poems onto the left half of a sheet of paper. They should add a drawing on the right half that illustrates the theme of their poem. Have them glue the poem onto a sheet of construction paper to give it a more finished look.

♦ Hang the poems on a bulletin board under a banner that reads I'M A POET, AND I KNOW IT.

Good Word of Mouth

Help students conquer their fear of public speaking by emphasizing the eight characteristics of good stage voice and presence.

Materials

* legal-size copy paper
* colored pencils
* scissors
* tape

Creating the Bulletin Board

♦ Give each student a sheet of legal-size copy paper.

♦ First, have students cut the paper in half vertically.

♦ Next, have them tape the two lengths together.

♦ Then, they should fold the strip of paper accordion-style so they end up with eight panels. To do this, they can fold the long strip of paper in half three times and open it back up to reveal the eight panels. They can use these folds as a guide to finish the accordion folds.

♦ With the accordion book folded together, have them draw in lines and then cut them as shown to create a paper-doll chain of drama masks. They can decorate the cover like a drama mask and add a title such as, "Robyn's Accordion Book of Good Stage Voice and Presence."

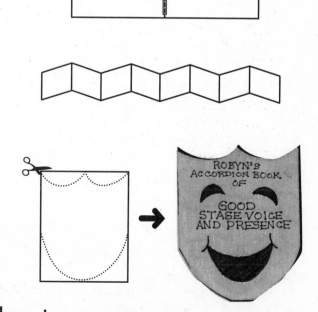

◆ Discuss the eight characteristics of good stage voice and presence (see below). On each of the eight interior panels of the accordion book, students will write the name of a characteristic and a sentence describing it, and they'll draw an icon that represents the characteristic. An icon is a simple image without words that acts as a mnemonic device to help students remember the characteristics. The icons should be as unique as possible. Icons tap into the strengths of visual learners. For instance, to illustrate *rate* students could draw a speed limit sign, a turtle, a heart monitor, or a racing car. To illustrate *clarity* they could draw a glass of water, a diamond ring, or a window pane.

◆ After students have finished their accordion books, hang them on a bulletin board under the title GOOD WORD OF MOUTH. Staple the first and last pages to the bulletin board so that the inside pages can be seen. Keep some of the accordion effect so it looks three-dimensional.

Eight Characteristics of Good Stage Voice and Presence

1. **RATE:** Most people speak too fast when giving an oral report because they are nervous. It is just as important to not speak too slowly.

   Encourage students to take three deep breaths before starting to speak. This helps calm them. You can also walk the class through visualization exercises. Turn off the lights and have them sit back with their eyes closed. Tell them to visualize that they've just run up a flight of stairs. Ask them what their heart rate would be like and how their breathing would be. As they relax, their heart rate slows, and their breathing becomes more steady. Then tell them to visualize a place where they feel at peace. This can help calm their nerves and improve their rate of speaking.

2. **PROJECTION:** Speakers need to project their voice so they can be heard.

   At the beginning of the year, try taking students into the gym and have them deliver their speech from the other side of the room. (Call this their "gym voice.") After returning to the classroom, tell them to use their gym voices whenever they speak too softly. This prompts them to speak loudly. They can exercise their diaphragms— the muscle which aids in projection—by saying, "ha-he-hi-ho-hu," several times quickly and forcefully.

3. **CLARITY:** Speakers need to enunciate and use good diction in order to be understood. Introducing students to diction exercises and tongue twisters is a good way to help them develop clarity in their speaking voices.

   Write a tongue twister on the board each day. When students line up or when they go to the rug for certain lessons, pick students to say the tongue twister three times very quickly. If they do it without stumbling they can line up or go to the rug. This turns diction exercises into a game, and students work on the daily tongue twister throughout the day in order to succeed.

4. **EXPRESSION:** Students need to vary their intonation when speaking in order to add character to their voice. This keeps their speech interesting.

Whenever reading to the class, overemphasize expression to show them how much fun it is to listen to an expressive speaker. You can try improvisation activities—acting out scenes from books or events from history—to make students more comfortable with being expressive. This translates into expressive oral reports.

5. **PITCH:** "Pitch" is the highs and lows of a person's speaking voice. Without a varied range of pitch, a speech will sound monotone and dull.

Vocal warmups are helpful before oral reports. For instance, students can say, "Aaaaaah," over a 10-second period, starting at the top of their register and sliding down into their lower register. Singing songs that have a wide range of notes is helpful—and fun.

6. **STANCE:** It is important to stand straight and tall and confidently when speaking. Do not sway, pace, rock, or cross your legs.

When students give an oral report, remind them to count silently to three before they begin, making sure they are standing with confidence. When they end their speech, they again count to three before sitting down. This prevents them from talking while they are getting into place or as they are finishing their presentation—another sign of nerves.

7. **EYE CONTACT:** Don't look at the ground or ceiling when speaking. Look at your audience.

Remind students to rehearse their speeches so that they know what they want to say. Being unprepared increases nerves and makes you want to look away from the audience. Suggest that they concentrate on the first few lines of their speech. Getting off to a good start increases confidence.

8. **POISE:** When a speaker makes a mistake it is important to recover quickly and continue, so as to not call attention to the mistake.

Show the class a videotape of an ice skater who has fallen. The skater gets up and continues with the program as if nothing happened. Then ask students to visualize what would have happened if the skater got up angrily and skated the rest of the program in that manner. The same is true with news anchors; if they stumble on a word they just continue with their report as if nothing happened. Stumbles and gaffs are forgotten if they are glossed over.

The Olde Time Radio Hour

Encourage creative expression by having students listen to an old radio show and adapt shows of their own.

Materials

* tape recorder
* blank tapes

* recordings of old radio shows
* Radio template (page 61)

* paper
* colored pencils

Creating the Bulletin Board

♦ Play excerpts from some old radio shows, such as mysteries, westerns, or comedies. They are usually available at the public library. Have students listen to the ways characters and settings are described, the sound effects that are used, and the background and theme music that is used. Compare the sound effects of a mystery with those of a western or comedy. Ask them to suggest ways the sound effects were made.

♦ Divide the class into groups. These groups will adapt a piece of writing for a radio broadcast. Consider using this as an author study (each group can adapt a different story). You can also have each group adapt a different chapter from a novel, write scripts as part of a genre study, or write radio newscasts set during a particular time period.

♦ When adapting their story into a radio script ask each group to use as much dialog as possible, eliminating the narration when they can. Have them find background and theme music. They should discuss the sound effects that their story needs and find ways to produce the sounds. Have a variety of musical instruments, wood blocks, boxes of pebbles, etc., available.

♦ Groups should record their radio shows. Then have the class listen to them. Encourage students to draw a picture of a main event from each story after listening to them.

♦ Groups can create a folio for their script with a cover illustration. Hang the scripts on a bulletin board, with the recording of the show in a ziplock bag underneath them. Students can listen to the radio shows at the listening center. Copy, color, and cut out the Radio template to hang on the bulletin board along with a banner that reads THE OLDE TIME RADIO HOUR.

We're All Thumbs!

Students are sure to give two thumbs up to this time line activity as they create thumbprint cartoons to illustrate their autobiographies.

Materials

- ❋ colored pencils or markers
- ❋ white construction paper
- ❋ scissors
- ❋ Time line template (page 64)
- ❋ ink pad
- ❋ tape

Creating the Bulletin Board

♦ Provide 2–4 copies of the Time line template for each student. Each template has four panels, and students will need one panel for each year of their life. So if a student is ten years old, he will need three copies of the template. He can discard two panels or share them with a classmate.

♦ Have students glue the templates to white construction paper. This prevents the ink from showing through and gives the project a more finished look.

♦ Have students cut each of the dotted lines on their templates, making sure to stop where the dotted line meets the solid line.

♦ They should fold the flaps down. The lines should be on the inside of the fold (figure 1).

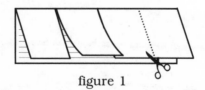

figure 1

♦ Students should place the panels horizontally in front of them so that the side with the flaps is facing down.

- Have them tape the right edge of the uncut panel to the left edge of the other one (figure 2). This should be done from behind so it doesn't cover the area where students will be writing. Students can add more panels, if necessary, to have one panel for each year of their life.

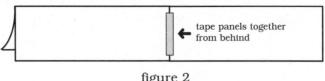

figure 2

- Students should brainstorm major events that happened during each year of their life. They might want to consult their parents for more information. Have students write a complete, detailed paragraph describing each event. They should write the paragraphs under the flaps on their time line, from left to right, starting from their year of birth up to the current year.

- Ask students to write the date of each event on the cover of the flap. The dates should be written at the bottom of each flap.

- Above each date, students should use an ink pad to make a thumbprint. They can use colored pencils or markers to make the thumbprints into cartoons of themselves experiencing the event. See the example below.

- After the students are finished with their time lines, hang them on a bulletin board under a banner that reads WE'RE ALL THUMBS!